"900 Words Can Explain Everything You Need To Know About Life"

By Don Tabler

**AUTHORED BY
DON TABLER
FOR HIS CHILDREN
GRANDCHILDREN
AND GREAT GRAND CHILDREN HERE
AND YET TO COME**

Foreword

Counter-intuitive is a strange word combination , … the opposite of what you might think… it happens in odd places and here are some of the most important to grasp:

1.) KEEP YOUR SUCCESS TO YOURSELF. I know how strange. Fact is you will never be a "blue jean " millionaire if the majority know you are doing well in your enterprise. If the hyena knows an easy meal, you are generally it.

2.) Never accept the credit when you did it right, always share it out with specific credit to, first the least deserving, then gradually to the most helpful, and emphasize that it was a successful group effort. That's how to lead from the front. Credit wont buy a cup of coffee.

3.)Try to maintain intellectual honesty with yourself. your reach should exceed your grasp, only after you are ready to reach, or it will end badly.

4.) Go to school to get A DEGREE, go to the library FOR EDUCATION. Fortunately today no subject is so abstruse that it doesn't have thousands who did it, and will share it.

5.) When choosing a mate don't jump at the first gold ring to appear, take real time to think about what will make you happy for the longest period of time, not this evenings 24 carat brass. Make this your first priority.

6.) Practice public speaking , no one is born comfortable with it, it takes real practice, Kipllng cautions *"Dont look too good, nor talk too wise:"*. At the same second don't hide your light totally under the bushel, balance and- questions asked- will make you a success in any endeavor.

7.) If you want a million dollars, gather ten thousand, a hundred k will follow, then the million thunder in, without trying. Opportunities arrive more frequently than bus lines.

Acknowledgments

*Today's poets write lyrics and become rich,
writing poetry in the past was a labor of love,
frequently seen as a Hallmark of the educated , it
occasionally made people money.
Desiderata is the most complete one page list of
how to live ever written,
If -Joseph Rudyard Kipling was written for his
son who was killed in the first world war
Invictus William Ernest Henley was written by a
person who overcame incredible personal
challenge and was written after the death of his
son
High flight as a pilot I adored this, the author
was killed in a training flight with fighters in
England shortly after this was penned to his
parents
The blind Men And the elephant is puckish
approval of ABSOLUTES*

INVICTUS William Ernest Henley

This poem is in the public domain. William Ernest Henley- William Ernest Henley, born August 23, 1849, was an influential British poet, perhaps best known for his poem "Invictus" (1875)

High Flight John Gillespie Magee, Jr
This poem is in the public domain. Magee, John Gillespie. "Letter to Parents," September 3, 1941

The Blind Men And The Elephant - Poem by John Godfrey Saxe
the poem itself is in the public domain

Dedication

I Find Myself Unexpectedly Surrounded By A
Loving Family,
My Spectacular Daughter Jessica Max, Her Two
Sons, Hunter And Holden, Their Children Gyntery,
Aspyn, And Swayde, Lots Of Daughters And Sons
Married Into The Family, And Even More
Grandchildren To Love And Entertain -This Book
Is Dedicated . And I Would Like To Thank A
Special Person,
Don Singletary, A Great Teacher, Who Has A
YouTube Free Course In Earning From
The Micro E Mini Investments, His Book "Day
Trading Micro Futures for Income"
Is At Amazon
He Took Time From A Very Busy Life To Give Me
Encouragement
And Suggestions Including The Title To This
Book

Table Of Contents

CHAPTER ONE
900 words on negotiating anything

I have done a huge amount of negotiating of purchases in my life time, while a lot were in flea markets about five hundred were for homes, apartment complexes, pools of mortgaged repos and a great many mobile homes that were abandoned. This information is being imparted *not* as the final word in how it's done, but as a lick and promise to the idea that I hope will help you.

1.) You Make Your Profit When You BUY, not when you sell or use. By law the worth of something is what happens when a willing buyer and a willing seller agree to the exchange of something. The key word here is WILLING. What you are looking for in any deal is- if you are the buyer- an unwilling seller. If the party is afflicted with foreclosure, divorce or health that threatens, he is an unwilling seller and that my dear is where the bargains lurk that will make you a realistic *guaranteed* profit.

In the circumstance of an individual who bought something with family money found himself unable or unwilling to complete his licensing, and now wants to flit away to some other activity whether oil or shaved ice, its time to issue a lone wolf call to the pack and set out to dine on a wounded elk. Some questions to ask anyone to determine if you should go into hunter killer mode:

2.) Have you spent any money on it recently?

You don't really care , but you have to get the party talking to see how they feel about it . When wanting to know if a no money down deal is possible, I always call rental owners and ask have you ever considered selling, if dealing with a seller of property, I always ask have you ever considered renting it?If the renter of property has considered selling -he will take a no money down deal. If the seller of the property has considered renting it, he too will take a no money down deal. Now obviously we are talking a first last and security deposit type of no money deal, but in either case what you are looking for is someone who is willing to carry the note. The seller is always the best source of finance, and if they wont finance the majority of it look again at what you are buying...

3.) A further consideration, if he wants his price, you get your terms, and vice versa. <u>Ask what he will do with the money,</u> if invest it and live off it-you can do better than a bank or savings and loan and if he isn't willing to do the deal you better look at what you are buying, **he knows what it's worth better than you do**... Being a good listener will make you a millionaire, so get them talking and shut up. if he wants to take the money and run-. into oil or a candy shop, he will take a very low price to get his candy fix. Keep rule one paramount here, other buyers are always ready to step in and buy without caring what the bones of the deal are, but the bones are the most important part of the process. Is it a good deal for you ...is your number one consideration. Deals that make both of you happy are possible, but always negotiate for your interests first..

4.) Jumping off places.
playing hardball start at two thirds
killing off a cripple go to one third or less
expect to strike a point at the 75% level only if its something that you really want.

5.) Always keep in mind that -"whats in it for you?", is a result of what you pay to buy it, not in the pie in the sky by and by. You can make 15% buying tax warrants on real property in Arizona, so you should look for a thirty percent minimum advantage as a rule of thumb when you're paying full price, extra work means extra people, office expense, supervision, etc. you will pay the price for not getting your price. Somewhere it has to come back to you .and if you are going to be one of the help you should get the helps price plus a spiff for supervision, paying the bills and furnishing the buy in.

Specifically in any deal.

Remember if he paid 175 for it he got some back during the time he ran it (or owned it) and it was never a deal where you can jump in and jump out. Now if he wants to go run after other things he shouldn't get the double dip of having pulled 50k out in salary and $225k. Too if he is going to pay off the debt to the family and re borrow it all again he shouldn't get enough to make the "jump of the day to the new brightly painted toy", are there other buyers willing to ignore the fact that he has obviously mis managed the thing he's selling and you will have to spend time polishing it back to luster... you bet . Don't be one of them, how much of what he is offering will be subject to attrition, so how much are you REALLY BUYING?

CHAPTER TWO
900 words on "Lies, Damn Lies, and Statistics"

Lies:

You may rest assured that most of what you have learned is wrong. Unfortunately most of what you have yet to learn is probably going to be wrong. Even worse, there really isn't a single touchstone you can bring to bear that will let you figure out for sure what is real and what is a fabrication. A charming fairy tale I recall is about the *Emperors New Clothes*, if you don't know it, find it and read it for you will find to your chagrin that you are the emperor -all too many times in your life time. That leaves you with a difficult path through the forest, without a trail of bread crumbs to follow. At this point you would be forgiven if you crawled under a large cardboard box and hid for the next seventy years. I saw a blind man this last week on TV that had lived till he was 6 without knowing he was blind. His parents had decided to let him live his life in the real world instead of telling him what was safe and right and proper. When playing baseball he kept hearing people talk about seeing the ball and discovered others have an ability he was born without. He was playing basketball and hitting nothing but air while he talked. He rode bikes, simply by putting a nylon wire tie around a lead bikes wheel so it clicked, he just followed the sound. He showed how to tell where a solid wall was by clicking his tongue   He had to figure out his way, without bread crumbs , and without a trail ... seemed happy with his life.

Damn Lies:
The most common liars you encounter will be in Government. Everything the Government says to you will not just be a lie, but a way to cheat you out of whatever you own, possess or earn. When this is pointed out to the government they call it spin doctoring, or send the person making the accusation to prison or a mental facility. On a scale of evil the government ranks about eight point seven on a ten point scale. Whenever government finds a new way to mess about with you they will get the support of local ministers in churches. Ministers universally are looked upon as honest citizens who deserve a ten percent discount on the whiskey they preach against for YOU. Teachers accept the lies they are given without question and pass it along to you with the requirement that you accept it as TRUTH. If they don't, they get fired. Look upon what you are getting from government as totally a fabrication designed to trick you and take everything you have, from ministers look at the way they live and then the way they tell you to live, and as for teachers, simple forgiveness for their lack of education seems an act of charity we can all strive for. Ministers peg a ten point scale of evil, teachers would bounce along in the low fours, they just follow and do what they've been told...

Its the same excuse the German Guards at concentration camps used when being hung, but at least its something.

STATISTICS:

Of all the means of sneaking stuff by you , the worst by far is statistics. Whenever you are told that 72% of the people asked said something was good for you or bad for you or correct, or desirable. put your wallet in your front pocket where it's harder to have it picked. If you get a chance ask carefully for the question that got the results, do it slyly and with tact for if alerted the quot-er of statistics is the most dangerous of the liars you are likely to encounter. The others will knife you if you're obvious in not believing their tripe, but the statistics quoters will torture you, and drag you to death behind their pickup truck, then provide written proof that 72% of the people approve of their deed. In the world you can get 18 to 22 % of the people to agree to anything no matter how impossible, unfair or evil it happens to be- by the way the question is written. If you ask someone a question for a survey, you will see that most people are being polite and trying to tell you what you want to hear, not what they actually think. So to skew the results just make it seem moral, right thinking or blessed by the majority. The purpose of this disclosure is to alert you that you are the one who must make your own way through far worse than a forest. Look for guidance in what you are told, seek info from books and research, but choose YOUR path carefully, with the best info currently available- and with full knowledge that you are guaranteed to have to change course without warning. Trust your gut instinct against any other information, idea or required belief. "Expect the UN -expected..".welcome to Reality 101. Finally don't loan money to a friend, make it a gift, gamble on *yourself* not what number will appear on a spinning wheel. The Jack Of Diamonds WILL jump out of the deck of cards and bite your ear, and in any business venture _nobody_ touches your money that's not blood.

CHAPTER THREE
900 words on finding your way

So- finding your way ... in the universe. The best advice anyone can give you is to find something you would do for free, and figure out how to make money at it. Like all simple truths, there is a large difference between hearing it, and putting it into an effective way to keep food on the table. Yet every year some person of average intellect looks at some common object and figures out how to improve it in a novel fashion, then gets big rich, Don't start out to make a million bucks by finding a way to take water and make money from it. I obviously grew up when no-one would have believed that water would sell for more than gasoline. Since it does, someone is making big money for it. So lets take a look at what could possibly be done to make money from water.

1.) How about doing some research on those packs that get really cold to help chill a sprain and find a way to put that into a bottle (sealed from the water) so that it would let you chill the contents of the bottle, how about flat bottles for easier storing in an ice chest? There
are already small filters for removing contaminating bacteria from water that can be purchased for ten bucks so people can drink from roadside ditches. Fact is you can take 4 inch PVC, and fill two four foot lengths with sharp clean sand

and another four foot piece filled with charcoal and in a space 12 inches by four feet , four inches thick you can make a filter for a house and sell it to those whose water is contaminated with bacteria, bad taste etc...all you have to do is find the right pieces of tubing to adapt it to water lines and you can sell one to anyone with a well.

 This is Water , which has been around for a long time, its a simple product, without it you will die, you have to learn to think about anything, as something that has stayed that way, not because it cant be improved, but because it just hasn't been done yet. To boil this down , write down ten simple items and put them into a hat and draw one out. See if you can find a way to make it simpler, better, or cheaper. If you do this in a group be sure you follow a simple plan , everybody has to have something to help, and speak out loud about their plan, and NOBODY can criticize that idea. You can springboard a solution from something completely un workable if you work to figure out how something Can be done- and forget about why it Can't be done.

 The ability to look at something, and come up with a way to make it feed you is important, but the fact is that you will find very little support for the concepts of ..."find a need and fill it." I used to have a business card that said ..."The thing that's free at the headwaters of the Orinoco River, is advice on why It wont work." Its a lot more complex an idea than it seems, for you can always find someone standing in the corners who will tell you why your idea, or your approach -wont work. What you need desperately is advice on how your idea can work. Keep the nay sayers out of the room whenever you're trying to find your way , that doesn't mean you should bet the house on your idea right out of the gate, it does mean that no matter how much someone wants you to succeed , they will find the dangers, difficulties , and impossibilities so overwhelming that they cant see how THEY would be able to do it. Irrelevant as it seems there's no truer statement than ..."an expert is someone who is thirty miles from home...". Don't just keep the nay-sayers out, throw them out and don't let them back.

3.)Obviously if you're going to take these chances you will want to plan for the eventualities, and obviously too you will find that no one can plan for everything that can go wrong. In every endeavor there comes a moment when its time to shoot the engineers, and get on with what needs to be done. Huge gains are impressive , and nearly impossible to attain, but break the concept into small parts you can attain, set a date to get there and accomplish that small goal without fail. Plan on paper for, ideas that aren't written down are fleeting, plans that aren't written down are like chewing gum for the mind. When I was in high school there was one boy who was awkward and gangling, he spoke reasonably well and had a positive manner about him. He was a popular young man because he worked hard at grades, went on the debate team. was always first to volunteer for fund raising and the scut work of setting up for dances or pep rallies. It was confided to me that he had a fairly low IQ. He didn't care, he excelled with the intellect he had and was successful in his life. Bloom where you are planted

Chapter Four
900 WORDS ON
Greasing the Wheels

I have always enjoyed learning from what I call "Folk Wisdom". The fables and tales told by the common people for entertainment and to make a point frequently have a truth that shines brightly and makes a difficult concept clear. One of these stories is about two lumberjacks who get into a contest to see who can bring down the most trees between sunup and sundown. One of the lumberjacks shows up at the contest convinced he will win and charges into the woods at first light he chops furiously and pauses to see if he can hear his opponent, when he hears nothing he smiles hugely and attacks the trees with fury. Finally he hears his opponent chopping in a different part of the forest and all day long he swings his axe without pause , while from the distance his opponent is taking timeouts and he hears no axe blows. The Sun goes down and he swaggers out to ask the judges how much he has won the contest by. He is told that he felled four trees an hour, and his opponent felled five and a half trees an hour. ..."But how can that be I heard him stopping all the hours we worked?... he asks. The judges shook their heads , "Your opponent," ... they said ..."took time to sharpen his axe."

You need to take time to sharpen your axe in whatever you do. Study the other ways to do what you are trying to do. You are generally better off to set up a group of persons with similar interest than to go it alone. If you are doing something worthwhile there's plenty of room in it for anyone who is competent. When I was young I read constantly, and was not looked upon as a potential friend by anyone. I felt isolated and unwanted . I found that if I could find something the other person did really well and ask them to show me how they did it, all of a sudden I was no longer viewed as threatening and was actually accepted.. It may come as a surprise to you that if you have a plan and are working to be successful, you will be viewed as threatening. Most people cannot motivate themselves without someone standing over them. Most people need an outsider to validate their thoughts, deeds and plans. Obviously Most people never rise to success and if you don't want to end up cutting logs with a dull axe, you have to learn to expect being isolated. Work out your own method of gaining acceptance. My method worked for me, offering help to them might work if it can be done with enough tact, for instance, if they are having trouble with something you find easy don't say ... that stuff is easy, say to them instead... "i notice you are having trouble with xxxxx and its about to eat my lunch, could we work on it together? I have some success with handling the problem like this but what you're doing looks a lot easier to me." Then shut up and let them contribute. You might just find an easier way to cut down trees. Learning from others is a way to short circuit the time it takes for you to become successful, but even more important it teaches You to be a leader, for a leader is what you have to be.

A great folk tale about leadership is about two bosses who needed to get a log chain moved to the top of a hill. one arranged everyone around the log chain and yelled at his employees ..." push you idiots push..." The other grabbed the end of the chain and started walking up the hill...."Little help over here " he asked quietly.

Your objective is always to get the log chain up the hill, how can you enlist the help of others to get it there. Lao Tzu was a master of the "Art of War" a book he wrote about two thousand years ago, says that a general is weaker for every man attracted to his banner. He was talking about the problems that come about when you have to wrangle not just yourself, but everyone around you. Other people wont understand your motivation to succeed, your long term goals, your methods, and the tools you use. As a leader you need to balance getting the chain up the hill with your method , and walking past and overriding an easier way to get it up the hill. If there's no real hurry about it, ask for an idea from everyone you have assembled on how to do it better. Indeed that's one of the best ideas for any leadership position , ask every one assembled for an opinion , don't let anyone criticize whats being said and make that clear up front. Then call on everyone assembled and require something from each, make it clear that if they have an idea that's different its not wrong, and might help everyone to do a better job, or faster or more economical job. Don't expect much the first time you do this, but make it clear that you're going to do this again next time. you are learning to lead by following the advice of the multitude and the multitude need never be reminded that *you* **chose** the direction, method and object of the travel.

Chapter Five
900 WORDS ON
Do It Yourself

The universe is a grand place to hang out. That's fortunate for alternatives are not readily found. You have a huge number of choices in what you can do where to go, how to live, but the universe has two things which it gives you no choice in.

1.) *You will become a mechanic.*
Yes if you have a car you will have to figure out some things or, be victimized by 17 year old boys who throw thousands of dollars of parts at a problem, until they finally hit on the right solutions. Fortunately many of the common problems with any car are fixable with little investment in the tools or parts. which leads us to the second choice that the universe requires of you.

2.) *You will learn to use a computer.* In order to fix the car (or anything else) just go to Google and type in a question exactly as you ask a person. Hit enter and in fractions of a second, you will have discussion groups, direct ideas, answers by the hundreds of thousands, a solution you can implement or hire implemented, while you watch. That means unfortunately that you must learn how to fix a computer, and that means you must have two computers so that when the first one is screwed up, you have something else to go to Google, and ask what to do . When you first consider getting a computer you will have to learn to type. There are great games that teach you to type.

The patience to start to understand the concept that a computer *doesn't* understand you, and you have to ask the right question, entered in a manner that the question is correctly typed. Misspelled words make the computer find stuff that has no relationship to what you asked-these are on you. So of the two things the universe requires of you, the one that's most important is the computer. You should be able to use a word processor which is what this is being written on, to write, correct, and cut and paste information. Fortunately almost every word processor is close to being the same so if you learn on the first one, you have any number of alternative ones. So lets be clear, you *will* learn to use a computer, and that means you have to learn to type. Now for the fun stuff, computers have all the TV programs ever broadcast to keep you entertained. Gooogle has every book ever written so there is no information, concept or novel you cant have delivered in fractions of a second. When you are learning don't neglect to learn how to use the Excel, Spreadsheet program. a spreadsheet is like the great wall of China, think of every brick in that wall stretching hundreds and hundreds of miles. ON EVERY ONE OF THOSE BRICKS YOU CAN ASK A DIFFERENT COMPUTATION TO TAKE PLACE.

This lets you find an answer to simple questions, and it insures you can make money by taking care of your own books when you get into business. Therefore you can figure out not just if you are making money, but how much as soon as something sells or is purchased. It also lets you make intelligent decisions on whether you should buy something, letting you figure how much you can make with the item, and forecasting how long the item will last. The spreadsheet is the greatest genie ever invented to make money for mankind and in spite of its imposing appearance, it is incredibly simple to use. You can use it to make decisions on investments, you can figure out mortgages for yourself, you can actually discount the mortgages you might want to buy for investment purpose, so that you aren't stuck with 1 or 2 percent rates of return, instead you can easily earn 15-25 % . Because some people need their money instantly, there's no shortage of great fixed rate returns that guarantee how much money you can make. You can get a great idea of how much, and when a stock is a great investment, and of whether you should or shouldn't buy it, all with the magic of a spreadsheet.

Learn to use the other great things a computer can do, and set up a Data system that lets you keep track of the name, address, phone number, and email address of people you know and meet. Then if you want to have a party you can write the letter of invitation, send it to everyone on the list, and everyone will get a personal invitation. Its in business that *comma separate values* or *comma delimited* information will make you rich, for you can find a list of persons, or companies, voters, leaders, followers or anything else. Its called a mailing list, and it lets you set up mass mailings, lists to call, people you should know, ask for help or advice, or how to information. For the first time you can have an idea on Monday, find someone to make the item you thought of on Tuesday, receive it back on Wednesday, find a place to manufacture your item on Thursday, sell it on Friday and deliver it on Saturday. There are in fact less jobs today than before, but there are more opportunities for a person to set up and run their own company today, than ever. The computer makes it possible to find other people who can help you find funding, set up companies, find homes, take vacations, work smarter and make more money than anything else you can do or own. Whether for fun or profit the computer is your personal slave.

Chapter Six
900 WORDS ON
Learn To Cook?

There is a great miracle in the simple preparation of food. Most people think that *gran cuisine* is filet *mignon.* Fact is any idiot can fix that cut of meat, bring me your rice and beans, fix that in a manner you would serve to the king... **that's** cooking. A woman I know once said that when a man smells onions cooking he thinks he is about to feast. So lets start with the most important aspect of cooking.

<u>Learn to sharpen a knife.</u>

Every onion should be first sliced , with a sharp knife from pole to pole. this keeps it from rocking around and getting you cut. Take off about a quarter inch end of both poles, then the paper coat comes off easily. Set the root end closest to you and holding the knife at a very shallow, angle make cuts from pole to pole, with the root end staying just <u>out</u> of the actual bottom of the cut. Then make cuts across the half and a miracle comes to pass, the little rings fall into tiny dice.

Saute the onions in a little olive oil or butter, this means cook them in a little butter over medium heat. The longer you cook them the darker they become, and the sweeter too. They also lose a lot of onion flavor when they are cooked for a long time, so use plenty. Onions are called aromatic, cause they have a large smell in anything. Garlic is easiest to get out of the little clump of individual cloves by smacking the whole bunch with your knife handle hard, then take the individual cloves, and smack them again with the side of the knife, they burst out of the wrapping paper they grew in and, you then use the flat of your knife to smack the naked little critter really hard and it turns to mush. You can make a few cuts across the mush to be sure you have the big chunks gone then, and only then add the garlic on top of the cut up onions in the pan. Don't let them get on the hot bottom, or they turn bitter. Add a palm full of oregano and two palms full of basil, a little fennel about the size of a stamp, and a little rosemary the same size, plus two cans of diced tomatoes, the big ones. Cook it on low heat, stirring frequently until its thick. You just made marinara for Italian anything. Now taste it for salt and pepper, and adjust to what you think is right, add it a little bit at a time.

You can cook spaghetti or pasta for about six minutes, in salted boiling water, and that's one great dish. Stir up about six eggs and cook them over low heat in a fry pan, add cooked bacon, cover with your sauce, add cheese, and you've made two great dishes. Cut a loaf of French bread in half, butter it, cook under the broiler for five minutes, top with the sauce -a grate of cheese, and you've made pizza. Wrap a cheap roast in aluminum foil slather with your sauce, slow roast it at 350 degrees in the oven for about 45 minutes, slice it thin, eat it with rice and you've made another dish. There are thousands of variations of the Italian sauce. and you learned the basic approach in thirty minutes.

I am telling you this in this place because there are many thing in your life that appear complex and melt into nothing if you take the first step. What you learn from your first attempts is how to magnify your result from a simple beginning. No matter what you choose to do to keep yourself fed and housed. Learn something simple, then learn to magnify the result. Recipe books can be found at the local Goodwill for a twenty five cent piece. Knowledge of how to make money costs little more, but after you find the book, go to Ebay and get it used. The knowledge inside the book hasn't lost anything just because someone else read it first.

Sharpen another knife...look for a niche market, find out how to use it to feed yourself, and get good at it. THEN go get an education in how to figure out the tatting patterns of the Guernsey Islands. You will have formed the habit of eating by the time you read this. You can always make a living if you can checker a gun stock, make a knife from a file, do scrimshaw, sew, make pots from clay, make glazes, fix air conditioners, fix a lawn mower, tan deer skins, buy hides, decorate leather, make a quilt, screen print, paint houses or a sunset. A great many people became rocket scientists only to find the trip to the moon was over, and they had to mow lawns for a living. If you become doctors you wont get to help people who need you, you will have to help people who can pay for the help, and get permission from a teenager miles away running a computer for the insurance company. There is an obligation to your future to look for a place of new beginnings. I think America still has the potential to be that place, but I see the door swinging shut on that future quickly. When the Soviet Union collapsed, it was there and feared one morning, and literally, gone the next day. If you think The United States is not in the same danger you are living in a lead mine.

Chapter Seven
900 WORDS ON
Investing Outside the Box

America creates millionaires at an astounding rate. We are still a country where someone can arrive on a boat with only a rag covering them, and ten years later- be appearing on late night television selling their course on how they made the millions. If you were to monitor the new millionaires in America you would find that of the next 100 millionaires who appear, 3 will **not** make their money in real estate. Because the people are touring the nation touting their course , which will set you back 3-10 thousand dollars you really should <u>attend their free seminar</u>, then NOT buy the extended version of the course, instead go to Ebay and buy their book, or course used. Most people who go to the seminars and get swept up in the excitement and enthusiasm then spend the money- lack the self confidence and ability to perform the actual action necessary to make the system work. I always say ...” money cant buy poverty...” Money also fails to give a person the major thing that makes it possible to put the idea into action which is a true commitment to making the system work.

The poem about the Twelve Blind Men and the elephant is a great one because each of the blindmen, feeling a different part of the elephant found a different animal .One found a tree, one a snake, one a fan one a wall type of animal. Taken separately they were all wrong but together they each found a part of the truth. Real estate is that way. No other investment opportunity provides more chunks of the animal wherein you can fetch up against the critter, and start making money. THE MORE YOU KNOW ABOUT WHAT THE ANIMAL LOOKS LIKE, THE MORE YOU CAN MAKE, AND THE FASTER THE MONEY COMES IN.

So you see an elephant, if you start at his feet and he looks like a tree you should also see papered there the beginners easy guide to making money called a fizbo.. FSBO is what it says or completely spelled out it says For Sale By Owner. It is certain that anyone can drive around ten minutes and find a sign that says for sale by owner. ***Look at one hundred of these before you make an offer.*** That many you say , Yep I answer, markets are all the same in most ways but unfortunately that sameness is all the way from a fabulous bargain to hopelessly overpriced money pits. You don't care- you are looking to build a knowledge of the bargains, and a feel for whats on the market.

After you find something on the market that strikes your interest, its time to move to the next stage, making the offer. A book by Paul Simon published in the eighties that actually teaches making offers is: *Make them an offer they cant refuse*. It taught me that the first thing is -never use the paperwork from a Realtor to make an offer That no Realtor is needed, wanted or desirable -in the process of making the offer. I searched for years for a copy of the book and finally found one, its been out of print for thirty years. I hope some day its re- issued for it has page after page of offers written in clear concise understandable language that were actually accepted. Its loose leaf, and you should read each of them, THEN gasp in amazement, for they will make you millions of dollars if you grasp one tiny thing. Make ridiculous offers... if they are all accepted you aren't doing it right, indeed you will make a million dollars if only one ridiculous offer is accepted out of 15. You can be assured that your capital needs to be used not on one project, but on several.

Keep your money to fix up your project, learn to do everything yourself, drywall, plumbing, painting, texturing, then do it yourself. If you get a nice property that needs a little fixing and do it yourself, you can sell it for less than the market for all cash or , sell it for ten thousand over the market by offering to carry the note yourself. Take enough money to make four payments on the house as down payment, and sell it on Contract for Deed. In the interest of keeping this somewhat short, the elephant has post it notes on every inch. Finding anyone of the post its and never doing anything else will make you really big money. Making the offer and getting it accepted is the most important part of the whole critter. For instance if you made the right offer, you can find someone to take over your position in the deal. You can pick up two to three thousand dollars, without spending a penny on the deal by adding- *and or assignee's-* to the offer. You sell it to someone else, and the deal still holds. By using the right weasel clause in the offer (*offer is subject to approval of all paperwork, by my partner, advice from my attorney or consultant etc)* you can duck out and not have an obligation to buy it.

Chapter Eight
How to KEEP What you Make
by
Getting Rid of It

Conventional wisdom teaches you that you should keep all your money in a conventional way. "Dont keep all your eggs in one basket..." is conventional, instead *keep* all your money in one basket *and watch the basket*. After you have made some serious coin, comes the question of how to handle it. THERE IS A DIFFERENCE BETWEEN WHAT YOU CAN SPEND AND WHAT YOU OWE TO YOUR CAPITAL. whoa wait a minute what the hell is my capital and why does he think I owe him anything? The fact is that making the really serious coin means having enough Capital to make it. It is hard to get together ten thousand dollars, easier to get together a hundred thousand, simple to make a million and the second million comes in less than 120 days. Capital that is , its impossible to make money that fast, so remember that the capital isn't yours . Ok -every third score you make , you get to keep half. Hows that?

You have to commit to your future and you have to plan how you are going to have a future, These plans need to be as previously stated, Written, NON WRITTEN PLANS ARE NOT PLANS THEY ARE A WHISTLING PAST THE GRAVE

YARD *MEANS*, OF AVOIDING SUCCESSES.
OK -Small steps you can attain, dates to complete
them , go kill the elephant one bite at a time...

So you did it. watch yourself- all of a sudden you
will be popular with strangers who want to get
what you've got, and will then leave with a
sucking sound like the road runner getting away
from Wiley Coyote. They are the least of your
problems for *government* will have alerted to your
success. Government employees feel anyone who
makes money is cheating the system, and needs to
spend time in jail. They go beyond an honest
chunk for services provided to wanting to punish
your accumulated funds *and* you , if possible, by
sending you to a galley where you get to be
chained to a bench and row all day long... without
TV. Instead they settle for just sending you to
prison and feel that taking all your money is part of
the game.

Don't deviate from this plan unless you want
fabulous abs and great biceps caused by eating
only gruel and rowing eight to twelve hours a
day. :
1.)Set up a corporation in Nevada. the corporation
is going to hire you for two hundred a week to do
whatever you do, the corporation will take all the
money you make and send it to an offshore trust in
one of the countries that currently have good
banking and tax law for money made offshore.

WAIT A FRICKEN MINUTE... you calmly announce at the top of your lungs, why would I give these foreign guys or the corporation my money? Answer. Cause you own the corporation, and the offshore trust, which you keep a deep dark secret. There was a time when you could put money in a sock in your sock drawer, but government is on to that dodge. They cant do anything about this one, its how Congress hides it's bribes.

Corporations LLC's,Partnerships,Sole Proprietorships, are agents of the state, they are granted by the state- for benefit of the state, monitored by the state, taxed by the state and you are going to do everything legal they require of any other corporation- including buying insurance on the worker (you) paying social security, and other taxes they come up with on the employee (you) and collecting income taxes from the employee on the $200 dollars a week they pay you. That way you get full coverage if something goes wrong and you get hurt or, if they still have it, some social security when you retire. Next the OFFSHORE trust... its not a creature of the state... it is a contract that sets up a means of handling money, property, cars, boats airplanes and all the trappings of wealth. ... as a disinterested party it is not you - *if* you make it an **irrevocable** trust, and make the beneficiary of the trust- another trust that is you. If its not an irrevocable trust (a revocable trust for instance) the government maintains that its just you hiding money, but wait you say if I give it to the trust isn't it gone forever, answer yes it is, but ... that's just the first layer.

You get to use anything the trust buys, this is the **beneficial interest**... like a new house or new car or airplane or boat and the trust like an indulgent rich uncle,pays for everything .... The items aren't yours , you just house sit for the trust... in any of three houses or more, you check out the maintenance level on the car, and the boat and airplane etc... all owned by the trust offshore- where there are no contingency fee lawsuits permitted.... Congratulations if you get sued -they can take everything you own... and nothing that you don't own- like the stuff in the trust... if you get attacked by the government hounds all they can get is your stuff, and the corporation ... which has sent everything offshore to a trust, and they get to keep the corporate documents in a large empty brown paper bag... When asked, the offshore trust that you set up, but don't appear in? It tells everybody to take a great flying etc and keeps whatever is left in the nation that doesn't have contingency fee law suits, and cant divulge documents... then sends you a free ticket on an airplane out of the country... to visit your money.

Chapter Nine
900 WORDS ON
problem solving
developing solutions to the insoluble

During world War Two, while we were bombing him, Adolph Hitler changed all German ground transportation (cars and trucks) to wood alcohol (kind you can't drink). Every American automobile manufactured for the last seventy years, for export to Brazil, has come from the factory ready to burn ethyl alcohol (kind you can drink). During the 1970's America had lines at filling stations due to a boycott by oil producing nations. Congress vowed a change and has performed so well that forty years later their committees are still urging a change to alternative forms of energy. Todays' solution from the hallowed halls is for drilling offshore to stick with petroleum as a primary energy source. Fact is that all American drilling rigs are tied up for the next 13 years and 38,000 acres of leased sites are yet to be explored. Makes Katrina response seem a model of efficiency. Yes today we have more fuel and sources, but its the same old stand.

"Fool me once shame on you , Fool me twice shame on me." Folk wisdom seems to be in short supply. There are solutions to all of Americas problems . Not just with energy, but with the loss of entrepreneurial starts, loss of manufacturing base and opportunity for all. We wont find solutions on Capital Hill. We can and should go back to our deep well of heritage. A concerted effort to provide Business Incubators, Risk Capital Venture Funding, requirements that local governments stand aside or provide alternatives for garage based business- mentoring from local successful individuals operating from enlightened self interest- and America can again rise as a nation of Yankee Traders. Cost of setting up a Hot Dog Stand in New York City currently exceeds sixty thousand dollars. Did you ever wonder where that nice Mr. Brown went after FEMA?

Energy: We already own the Interstate Highways, every mile could take a Wind Tower, grass clippings from mowing (straw, wood trimmings) makes wood alcohol when its heated in a closed container and condensed, or ferments with special yeast into grain alcohol. Compressed Natural Gas from your own garage would cost sixty cents per gallon, already in use in Police fleets in Phoenix costs of conversion are way less that 200 gallons of regular gasoline. We could replace all foreign oil imports with these methods in three years The danger is that just this *threat* will cause prices to fall in the petroleum fields....at least till the next time.

You need to question what you've learned and what you believe to be true. At any given time there will be insoluble problems waiting for you to take a quick look at them, obviously looking at them, and thinking of them in the same fashion using the same facts, isn't going anywhere very fast . Let's look at how to start to think yourself. What would happen if we were to put this question, not to the experts scratching their private parts in lost reverie, and instead- went to all our nations fifth grade classes and posed a question to them|? There would have to be a reward in the "contest" to solve the questions of :

      1.what to do with the mountains of used tires we generate daily.

      2. what should we do with the children taken from their parents and placed with the state?

      3. how to make taxes fair?

      4. how to do away with taxes?

      5. what can we do about religious cults?

      6. what will insure our citizens are represented in legislation, and not just pressure groups?

      7. your suggestion of an impossible?

      8. ditto

      9.ditto

      10.ditto

How would you set up such a project so it would work, and not cost the Government a thing?

We permit every fifth grade class in America to come up with a solution to one of Americas problems. Contest rules say every student in the class has to come up with an idea on how to confront it. The rule is, nothing is mocked or made fun of. The students will vote on which idea to pursue and tell why and how. Their ideas will be posted on a national site. First prize will go to the top ten classes in each category, chosen by popular national vote, all students in those classes receive a four year scholarship to college,, second prize 2 year scholarships, third prize one year scholarships, fourth prize 1000 dollars to the school where the students go, fifth prize 100$. Sixth through tenth honorable mentions, and ten dollar gift certificates from Mcdonald's . Every problem tackled is its own category. Government provides the money for the web site where the idea is posted, solicits contributions to pay for the rest. Total cost to the government less than two hundred dollars.

Now.... we have led the horse to water and we made him drink. next we get the horse and government to float on its back. Indeed asking government to solve problems is whats led us here... but think of the response this would have on the Nation. Someone somewhere would take the ideas from the group of children old enough to understand , but un- corrupted with the reality of impossibility... someone would take those thoughts and act upon them. So why not you? The Chinese say..." the longest journey starts with one step."

Chapter Ten
900 WORDS ON
How to survive thinking for yourself

Throughout history, poverty is the normal condition of man. Advances which permit this norm to be exceeded- here and there, now and then- are the work of an extremely small minority, frequently despised, often condemned, and almost always opposed by all right-thinking people. Whenever this tiny minority is kept from creating, or (as sometimes happens) is driven out of a society, the people then slip back into abject poverty. This is known as "bad luck." -- Robert A. Heinlein

If hypocrisy were suddenly worth anything, we would all be multi-millionaires. Don Tabler

Our nation survived two wars against the British Navy through the ability to issue what were called Letters Of Marque. These letters let private citizens outfit a small ship with cannons and set forth to prey on the un-armed civilian shipping of England. They were not Pirates (Aaaargh!) , they were Privateers (pass the stolen crumpets).

The history of Africa is remarkable. First they co operated in the sale of their citizens to foreign countries as slaves, then when the industrial revolution made that expensive, they were conquered by all the nations of the earth, their raw materials stolen for transshipment to *civilized* nations. The citizens of Africa endured this assault, and when the raw materials started to require real labor/money to recover, they were granted Independence... which means left to their own un educated, UNFUNDED devices. This occurred just in time to get caught between, America and The Soviet Union in a toss up that let their warlords get massive amounts of free weaponry, draft children into vast armies capable of destroying the weak unarmed, in record numbers and unprecedented ease.

Iceland, that tiny nation in the Atlantic, raised its offshore fishing limits to several hundred miles, where they routinely confiscate fishing vessels and fishermen who violate their expanded territorial limits. They release the ships and men after payments of huge fines. This is called punishment.

Somalia is located close to the outlet of the Suez Canal. The private citizens of the nation, left in abject poverty by the depredations of all the nations of the earth, acting with the tacit and unstated approval of whatever collection of corrupt individuals govern the wreck, get into tiny boats with automatic weapons and rocket propelled grenades, go catch un-armed freighters close to their shore. This is called Piracy, and is opposed by all right thinking nations and parties.

Africa has huge reserves of all those items needed in great profusion for manufacturing, and no means to use them. Africa also has an epidemic of AIDS which affects 65% of its people. The number one crop raised on the continent is Orphans. There is at the end of ten-hundred years of exploitation almost no infrastructure, no real education, no adequate health care , or potable water. That this rich stew of the disaffected and uneducated is a great recruiting ground for the Taliban and Terrorists, and horrid disease constitutes what would have to be called
 "***Really*** Bad Luck"
Water can be super cooled in a refrigerator to a point where it ,remains liquid at 30 degrees, without actually turning to ice. If suddenly it is given a whack it mysteriously turns solid in a most amazing display. Hopefully by this time in this book you have realized that many of the platitudes you've grown familiar with, are the simplistic mouthing of idiots. This is a dangerous turn of events, for nothing is less likely to endear you to those surrounding you, than recognizing that Oz, the great and powerful ...might be the little man behind the curtain, and not the apparition on the huge screen before you. This will cause you to feel alone and lost... rudderless and outcast. All of which is true when discovered, and equally true when you were un- enlightened. The fact is that the universe really is out to get you, but like a great

white shark biting you, there's nothing personal in the attack. You are walking around in all the security you will ever have and that has to be a frightening realization. *I wish I could assure you that it will get better, that the existence you live would provide you with warmth , home made soup and a fire to set beside when you grow old. But the facts legislate against it.*

Instead let my give you the whack named above, and assure you that your responsibility to think for yourself, seize your own destiny, find a path 'overaroundunder or through'... is yours and yours alone. You wont always choose correctly in love, friends, jobs, education, drugs, alcohol, ideal weight ,when to rise and greet the new day, what kind of dog to get or any other choice- for choice is freighted down with risk. True beauty lies in the eye of the beholder, truth is always lurking out there somewhere, unless of course you are afflicted with politicians. newsmen, gypsy contractors, self ordained ministers and others in the trade.

 So how can you proceed? Planning of course- and limiting un realistic expectations, such as constant success, doing the right thing because you have consulted the oracle or other wise party. "There comes a time in every job when its time to shoot the engineers and get on with the project.." In sales they speak about paralysis through analysis. Certainly it is necessary to work hard, even more necessary to work smart , but many people permit themselves to become so frozen with fear of making a mistake, that they never proceed with anything they undertake. A great truth is that any choice is better than no choice at all. If you chose wrong. you learned and that makes it a correct choice in anyone's book -for you learned what not to do.

Chapter 11
900 WORDS ON
Where the magic bullet lives

There are many myths we grow up with. Some of these are relatively harmless, (ie) red suited portly men with bags full of toys, magic sleighs, winged creatures with a desire for a bag of our old teeth and a purse filled with money that appears under our pillow. Other myths are inculcated into us as children and on a daily basis as adults. There is a myth of sanity, actually there's no such thing, there's only the ability to cope, and the inability to cope. There's the myth of the perfect child (if only you raise the child in this fashion, you get a perfect child). There's not yet been a perfect child, and wont be in any foreseeable future. These myths do a lot more harm than good

That having been said, and not intended in any way as a full and complete accounting, when raising a child you have a choice of where to put the failings. In expectation of a universe of daily unearned reward seems popular. The ever popular free ride through the universe is supposedly gifted to celebrities, intellectually gifted, and the wealthy. Fact is the universe really is out to get you, there's just nothing personal in it. Parents raised you to excel and for the most part, you do, and need make no apology for that. The failing inherit in this method is an expectation that you can control the universe and obviously, you cant. Therefore you accept responsibility for things outside your control. A search for eternal perfection is Marleys' Chain to drag . Learning to function with reasonable expectation of success is a defense. There are no happy choices, so everyone has to take what joy we can, in our success, cut ourselves some slack at our failings, recognize that we have a right to be here, and as far as possible be gentle with yourself.

So how do you proceed? By planning of course- and limiting un realistic expectations, such as constant success, great truth is that any choice is better than no choice at all. if you chose wrong. you learned, and that makes it a correct choice in anyone's book -for you learned what not to do.

 Economists have a golden rule that translates freely as ... "pay no attention to the man behind the curtain." The number of conflicting views of past economic debacles and future economic certainties serves only to keep thousands of government employees off the dole. The viewpoint of experts is pretty well moot to those of us who have to prosper on our own. Humanity has always been able to find, at the headwaters of the Orinoco River, advice on why something cannot be done; and always had to compensate an answer as to how it *could* be done with some item of value.

True beauty lies in the eye of the beholder, truth is always lurking out there somewhere,- unless of course you are afflicted with politicians. newsmen, gypsy contractors, ministers, and others in the trade. Thinking outside the box is not an option. For persons who want to survive, finding out how to do the impossible is always rewarded with the same urgency as your next breath. Fear of failure is ridiculous, if you tried something and it didn't work, you now can try the opposite direction. Horse shoes teaches anyone that you can get closer to an answer only by actually throwing the horse shoe, not by hiring an economist or farming out the grunt work of making your plan.

A wonderful curse that is truly frightening is the Chinese ..."May you attain that which you most fervently desire." With that caution in mind, you have to plan for several fronts at one and the same time and no one has ever done that before you ....all the time and in all cases. So let us begin at the beginning which you will find difficult if not impossible- unrewarding and dull as dishwater to endure....

       1.)What do you want personally : list at least five things, make them specific.

       2.)What do you want professionally : list at least five things, make them specific.

       3.) What do you want spiritually: list at least five things, make them specific.

Write these three down on three sheets of paper, under them write how you are going to proceed towards the goal, divide this journey into parts and assign a target date to each of them. Keep in mind some advice from Sigmund Freud. He was asked once how he chose between things when he didn't have any real preference towards either item. He said…"It's easy , I flip a coin." The asker of the great man was incredulous, …"How can you do that its so easy , what if your coin toss isn't what you really want." "That's the beauty of it"…Freud smiled…"If I don't like what the coin says, I just do the opposite." If you take away nothing else from this advice, take this. A plan has to be written, if its not written it's no plan at all. You are able to overcome any obstacle, fight any foe, achieve any goal if you will use your brain to write out a plan for getting there, if its not written- its not a plan. Then *work* your plan

Chapter 12
A Box Of "NON Chewing Gum"

Thinking outside the box is such a tired, over used and hopeless phrase . I have avoided mentioning this solution *sounding* phrase as much as possible, and simply demonstrated the concept. If you need to move a log chain you were given a phrase that works, (...little help over here...). un noticed in that was the concept that you lead from the front. All kinds of impossible solutions that were perfectly obvious when mentioned, were mysteries till pointed out. There's nothing in the world simpler than doing what you know how to do. So I sneaked a batch of things through your brain in an obvious) after the fact) manner. I hope I got though to you , that sometimes good people tell you the wrong thing, so:

Since self help books always end up simply hanging around, and helping not at all. I thought we might change that method of <u>chewing gum for the mind </u> and instead do something for the reader to repay such diligence. How about we play a game of *non chewing gum* "for the mind", about who you are, who you want to be, how to get there, and while we are at it, pick one of - five out of ten insoluble problems in the world- and fix that too. Follow instructions and playing one game will change your life for the better, that's from one time, there are no fees charged for multiple use.

The rules of NON Chewing Gum game are simple, and while you can play it by yourself at a stop light, or waiting for an airplane, or a meal to arrive, it's a lot more fun and instructive to play with from five to twenty persons, and the game has a no limit reward attached, just for playing it one time. So that you can't be intimidated about your chosen items for you, lets start with the problems of the world. Here are the first insoluble problems to choose from, they are not in short supply- so , expect a constant resupply.

To your assembled multitude the rules must be explained. "Fear of failure is ridiculous, if you tried something and it didn't work, you now can try the opposite direction." First read to the group the problems nobody can solve, I chose these for you to work on, but that's not the rule, if you want others, go for it. The group should choose one of the following:

     1.what to do with the mountains of used tires we generate daily.
     2. what should we do with the children taken from their parents and placed with the state?
     3. how to make taxes fair?
     4. how to do away with taxes?
     5. what can we do about religious cults?

Everybody has to have a suggestion, nobody can criticize it, anybody can spring board from it to another suggestion , and indeed the springboard itself is something to grow from. Re affirm, nobody can criticize anybody else input, even a dumb idea is an idea, and therefore helpful. Explain that concept to your group, and, bad news , you have to be the one to change this from a waste of time to something that will help, teach and instruct. Write it down "for a plan to work , it has to be written down". If you are reading this as an "e pub" you have to get a writing instrument, sheets of paper and follow the inputs on top of each sheet provided with the published book., if you have the book, there are pages provided for the game players

RULES CANNOT BE CHANGED!

If you play the game one time- as proposed, just one time, you will know more about running an organization than Harvard will teach in four years, and if you think about that statement and learn from it, lets do the really hard one that you hoped I would forget.

"1.)What do you want personally : list at least five things, make them specific.

2.)What do you want professionally : list at least five things, make them specific.

3.) What do you want spiritually: list at least five things, make them specific.

Write these three down on three sheets of paper, under them write how you are going to proceed towards the goal, divide this journey into parts and assign a target date to each of them.

.Chapter 13
Revisiting the Royal Nonsuch

These scribblings are intended primarily for the children, grandchildren, and great grandchildren of two persons, and none the less, it is inevitable that they will sneak out, and be discovered by a multitude. We can sense the horde gathering now in the dim fog of future un-formed memories, an assembled multitude carrying over ripe tomatoes, rotten eggs, tar and feathers. Therefore we erect at this site a solemn oath to appear , Wednesday evening as promised- in the final showing of The Royal Nonsuch, NO WOMEN AND CHILDREN ALLOWED , -- *special ten percent discount to law enforcement and clergy.* Huckleberry and Jim are readying the raft even as we scratch out this final chapter for their and your perusal. Other parties have conveyed a great many items of note- which will hopefully distract the mob long enough for us to shove off, and count our ill gotten gains.

Desiderata --- *Max Ehrmann, 1927*
Go placidly amid the noise and the haste, and remember what peace there may be in silence. As far as possible without surrender be on good terms with all persons. Speak your truth quietly and clearly; and listen to others, even to the dull and the ignorant, they too have their story.

Avoid loud and aggressive persons, they are
vexations to the spirit.

If you compare yourself with others, you may
become vain or bitter; for always there will be
greater and lesser persons than yourself. Enjoy
your achievements as well as your plans. Keep
interested in your own career, however humble;
it is a real possession in the changing fortunes of
time.
Exercise caution in your business affairs, for
the world is full of trickery. But let not this
blind you to what virtue there is; many persons
strive for high ideals, and everywhere life is full
of heroism. Be yourself. Especially do not feign
affection. Neither be cynical about love; for in
the face of all aridity and disenchantment it is
as perennial as the grass. Take kindly the
counsel of the years, gracefully surrendering
the things of youth.
Nurture strength of spirit to shield you in
sudden misfortune. But do not distress yourself
with dark imaginings. Many fears are born of
fatigue and loneliness. Beyond a wholesome
discipline, be gentle with yourself. You are a
child of the universe, no less than the trees and
the stars; you have a right to be here. And
whether or not it is clear to you, no doubt the
universe is unfolding as it should.
Therefore, be at peace with God,
whateveryou conceive Him to be. And whatever

your labors and aspirations in the noisy
confusion of life, keep peace in your soul. With
all its sham, drudgery and broken dreams; it is
still a beautiful world. Be cheerful.
Strive to be happy.

IF

If you can keep your head when all about
you
Are losing theirs and blaming it on you,
If you can trust yourself when all men doubt
you
But make allowance for their doubting too,
If you can wait and not be tired by waiting,
Or being lied about, don't deal in lies,
Or being hated, don't give way to hating,
And yet don't look too good, nor talk too
wise:

If you can dream--and not make dreams
your master,
If you can think--and not make thoughts
your aim;
If you can meet with Triumph and Disaster
And treat those two impostors just the same;
If you can bear to hear the truth you've
spoken
Twisted by knaves to make a trap for fools,
Or watch the things you gave your life to,
broken,

And stoop and build 'em up with worn-out tools:

If you can make one heap of all your winnings
And risk it all on one turn of pitch-and-toss,
And lose, and start again at your beginnings
And never breath a word about your loss;
If you can force your heart and nerve and sinew
To serve your turn long after they are gone,
And so hold on when there is nothing in you
Except the Will which says to them: "Hold on!"

If you can talk with crowds and keep your virtue,
Or walk with kings--nor lose the common touch,
If neither foes nor loving friends can hurt you;
If all men count with you, but none too much,
If you can fill the unforgiving minute
With sixty seconds' worth of distance run,
Yours is the Earth and everything that's in it,
And--which is more--you'll be a Man, my son!

--Rudyard Kipling

INVICTUS
Out of the night that covers me,
Black as the Pit from pole to pole,
I thank whatever gods may be
For my unconquerable soul.

In the fell clutch of circumstance
I have not winced nor cried aloud.
Under the bludgeonings of chance
My head is bloody, but unbowed.

Beyond this place of wrath and tears
Looms but the Horror of the shade,
And yet the menace of the years
Finds, and shall find, me unafraid.

It matters not how strait the gate,
How charged with punishments the scroll.
I am the master of my fate:
I am the captain of my soul.

William Ernest Henley

High Flight

John Gillespie Magee, Jr
Oh! I have slipped the surly bonds of earth,
And danced the skies on laughter-silvered
wings;
Sunward I've climbed, and joined the tumbling
mirth

Of sun-split clouds, --and done a hundred things
You have not dreamed of --Wheeled and soared and swung
High in the sunlit silence. Hov'ring there
I've chased the shouting wind along, and flung
My eager craft through footless halls of air...
Up, up the long, delirious, burning blue
I've topped the wind-swept heights with easy grace
Where never lark or even eagle flew --
And, while with silent lifting mind I've trod
The high untrespassed sanctity of space,
Put out my hand, and touched the face of God.

The Blind Men And The Elephant - Poem by
John Godfrey Saxe

It was six men of Indostan, to learning much
inclined,
who went to see the elephant (Though all of
them were blind),
that each by observation, might satisfy his
mind.

The first approached the elephant, and,
happening to fall,
against his broad and sturdy side, at once began
to bawl:
'God bless me! but the elephant, is nothing but
a wall!'

The second feeling of the tusk, cried: 'Ho! what
have we here,
so very round and smooth and sharp? To me tis
mighty clear,
this wonder of an elephant, is very like a spear!'

The third approached the animal, and,
happening to take,
the squirming trunk within his hands, 'I see,'
quoth he,
the elephant is very like a snake!'

The fourth reached out his eager hand, and felt
about the knee:
'What most this wondrous beast is like, is
mighty plain,' quoth he;
'Tis clear enough the elephant is very like a
tree.'

The fifth, who chanced to touch the ear, Said;
'E'en the blindest man
can tell what this resembles most; Deny the fact
who can,
This marvel of an elephant, is very like a fan!'

The sixth no sooner had begun, about the beast
to grope,
than, seizing on the swinging tail, that fell
within his scope,

'I see,' quothe he, 'the elephant is very like a
rope!'

And so these men of Indostan, disputed loud
and long,
each in his own opinion, exceeding stiff and
strong,
Though each was partly in the right, and all
were in the wrong!

So, oft in theologic wars, the disputants, I ween,
tread on in utter ignorance, of what each other
mean,
and prate about the elephant, not one of them
has seen!
John Godfrey Saxe